FADING DREAMS
AND
RISING FEARS

AMERICA ON THE EDGE

ROBERT MILLER
HENRY PARK

FADING DREAMS
AND
RISING FEARS

AMERICA ON THE EDGE

Copyright © 2020 by Robert Miller and Henry Park

ISBN 978-0-9975887-3-6

ALSO BY ROBERT MILLER AND HENRY PARK
C19 Economics

ALSO BY ROBERT MILLER
Rainmaking
The Magic of Selling
Second Wind

*To all those who have given
their blood, sweat, and tears to
make America great.*

PREFACE
By Robert Miller

In the end, we will remember not the words of our enemies, but the silence of our friends.

— Martin Luther King Jr.

Before we were attacked by the China virus, I thought I had seen it all. A baby boomer, my life has touched eight decades of the American Experience — from the first Cold War to the current one. America is on the edge — let's come together to end the pandemic, restore law and order, and save the American Dream.

A few weeks ago, when Henry Park and I published *C19 Economics: Your Guide to Personal and Business Finance* we had no plans to author this book. After watching a couple of weeks of Helter Skelter on the streets of America's cities Henry and I decided to write *Fading Dreams and Rising Fears*.

Fifty years ago, I asked a 17-year-old at Boston State College "what do you think about America?" Without hesitation she replied, "America is my country, I love her." I have often thought about those simple words "America is my country, I love her."

I love America. I always have and I always will. It tears me apart to see what is going on these days. The pandemic is one thing — it will eventually end one way or another. But the civil unrest — the anarchy that threatens our freedom, safety, and security — must be stopped.

— Robert Miller
Irvine, California
September 10, 2020

FADING DREAMS
AND
RISING FEARS

AMERICA ON THE EDGE

CONTENTS

This book is written raw and unplugged and is based entirely on our subjective opinions. There is no intent to be either politically correct, politically incorrect, or necessarily controversial. It reflects our present recollections of experiences over time. Some names and characteristics have been changed, some events have been compressed, and some dialogue has been recreated. This book has not been fact-checked so do your own due diligence. Feel free to cancel any of the content presented herein. If you choose to burn your copy of this book, please do so responsibly.

ONE
YOUR VOTE MATTERS

The ignorance of one voter in a democracy impairs the security of all.

— John F. Kennedy

There are many ways to make an impact on society — to change the things we do not like about America and protect the things we cherish.

Become an informed voter and make your vote count — all votes matter.

YOUR VOTE MATTERS

Your vote matters because, in the final analysis, it may be the most valuable thing you can do to influence the future of America.

Voting is more than a right — much more — it is a responsibility. That means that we have the responsibility to invest whatever time and energy is required to make the most informed decision possible.

The psychology of voting is extremely complex. Unfortunately — perhaps even tragically — many people will be casting their vote based almost entirely on emotional factors.

Electing the President of the United States should not be like electing the homecoming king or queen. Personalities should not matter much — looks should matter less. What matters should be who will best lead our country for the next four years.

This book will help you step back and take an analytical approach to deciding who will be the best president.

Let's take a look at how this book unfolds. The next chapter — **Chapter Two | Fading Dreams** — looks at America's back pages since World War II to discover the reasons our dreams are fading.

In **Chapter Three | Rising Fears** we look at the events that have unfolded over the past few months — the pandemic and the domestic terrorists threatening our country.

Chapter Four | On the Edge brings us to ground zero — the state of the union just a few weeks before what may be the most important election of our lifetimes.

After reflecting on the past and reminding ourselves where we are presently, we are going to consider some viable solutions in **Chapter Five | Saving the Dream**.

The issues are presented for your consideration in **Chapter Six | Election**. There 19 sections on what we believe are the biggest issues. There may be others that interest you. Invest the time to decide what is important to YOU.

3

We summarize our thoughts in **Chapter Seven | Back to the Future**. And that is what this book is all about — waking up from this nightmare and moving on.

Keep in mind that this is your book — use it as a workbook to help you decide how you are going to vote and why. Mark pages, use a highlighter, turn down page corners, and make notes wherever you want.

Take our lead but do your own research regarding the candidates and the campaign issues. Google the issues and be sure to visit as many sites as possible including the official sites of both candidates.

How are you going to make your decision about where you will place your vote? Are you going to vote for the candidate who believes the way you do about the role of government? Or will you vote for the one who agrees with your personal views of the issues? Will you vote for the candidate who best knows how to end the pandemic, restore law and order, and save the American Dream?

4

YOUR VOTE MATTERS

Endorsing **representative democracy** is voting for the candidate who shares your vision of the role of government. This is what Republican President Abraham Lincoln said about the role of government: **"The legitimate object of government is to do for a community of people, whatever they need to have done, but can not do, at all, or can not, so well do, for themselves — in their separate , and individual capacities."**

Endorsing **guardianship democracy** is voting for the candidate you believe is best capable of leading the country. Often this is based on a candidate's past performance.

Most people vote based on their political affiliations — Republican or Democrat — because of party platforms. This is usually the easiest way for a voter to decide.

This time more than any time in history, many voters make their decisions based on personalities. Many people will be voting for or against Donald Trump or Joe Biden for reasons other than political — that is why it's important to look at the issues.

Hold on to your dreams.
Reach for the stars.
Color outside the lines.
Dance on the edge.
Wash your hands for lunch.

TWO
FADING DREAMS

And I don't know a soul who's not been
    battered
I don't have a friend who feels at ease
I don't know a dream that's not been
    shattered
or driven to its knees

               — *American Tune* (1973)
               Paul Simon

Every moment dreams fade away and new ones appear. Hold on tight to your dreams — all of them — they may be all you have.

FADING DREAMS

Let's look back at the American experience — remembering that we evolved since people first arrived in America by walking across an ice bridge. 25,000 later people are still walking to America. Some of them have survived a 15-hour train ride from the northern border of Guatemala atop a train called *La Bestia* (the beast).

The tablet in the left hand of the Statue of Liberty carries this inscription: **Give me your tired, your poor, Your huddled masses yearning to breathe free, The wretched refuse of your teeming shore. Send these, the homeless, tempest tossed to me, I lift my lamp beside the golden door!**

America was **The Land of Dreams**. People from hellholes around the world risked their life savings and lives to come to America — legally or illegally. Some came in container ships and others crawled across the border in tunnels or floated here on inner tubes. Others paid smugglers to help them across the scorching deserts to have a chance at the American Dream. Others were brought here as slaves as we have been reminded.

FADING DREAMS

The naiveté of Americans began to fade in the early sixties with the Bay of Pigs Invasion and the Cuban Missile Crisis — and ended abruptly with the assassination of President John F. Kennedy.

The fifties were amazing years for America. We were on top of the world. We were proud to be Americans — extremely proud. We stood up and placed our hands over our hearts for the playing of the national anthem and reciting of the Pledge of Allegiance. We believed in America.

What can we do to save the American Dream? If there are answers to our current crisis, they are to stop allowing fear to control our actions, to believe in ourselves unequivocally, and to believe in God. Let us stop looking backward and being shamed into feeling guilty. Let us start dreaming again.

What is the American Dream and how has it changed? The American Dream has not changed much in the last four hundred years — but it seems to be fading.

FADING DREAMS

We all have our own version of the American Dream. Traditionally the American Dream is the belief that hard work will make you rich. And that is a problem because it is not about hard work.

We will talk more about the American Dream in Chapter Five | Saving the Dream. For now, let us think about how dreams are fading for most of us because of the pandemic shutdown.

You cannot work hard to achieve the American Dream if you do not have a job. The pandemic has turned many of us into zombies. And zombies cannot realize the American Dream.

We are weeks away from the election and the bottom line is that the future of the American Dream will be determined by who we elect as president.

For many the American Dream depends almost entirely on the economy. Without wealth it is usually hard to realize health and happiness. So, the economy matters.

FADING DREAMS

A respectable job, education, home ownership — maybe even owning a business — these are all some American Dreams. These dreams are fading away. For some it may only be temporary — a job furlough or temporary layoff.

For others, dreams may have already faded into oblivion. Many have lost their jobs forever as companies have permanently closed or scaled back.

Regardless of who is elected president we are in for some tough times — it is going to get much worse before it gets better. In our book *C19 Economics* we talk about the challenges and opportunities that will present themselves as the nation reopens.

Where there is crisis there are unlimited opportunities. This time is no different. Maybe it is all right to let some dreams fade. As some dreams fade, we will create new ones.

Fading dreams are okay but rising fears are not — let's learn about them now.

(Burn baby burn)
Burn that mother down y'all
— Disco Inferno (1976)
The Trammps

THREE
RISING FEARS

America was not built on fear. America was built on courage, on imagination, and unbeatable determination to do the job at hand.

— Harry S. Truman

The evil forces are doing everything they can to paralyze America — from forcing us to cover our faces to closing our businesses and schools — from rioting and looting to trying to shame is into cancelling our culture. Trump is not buying into fear.

RISING FEARS

This is a good time for us to pause for a few minutes and reflect on what Franklin D. Roosevelt said in his first Inaugural Address on March 4, 1933:
So, first of all, let me assert my firm belief that the only thing we have to fear is ... fear itself — nameless, unreasoning, unjustified terror which paralyzes needed efforts to convert retreat into advance. In every dark hour of our national life a leadership of frankness and of vigor has met with that understanding of support of the people themselves which is essential to victory. And I am convinced that you will again give that support to leadership in these critical days.

Fears are rising in America as we continue to be under attack from the deadly China virus and domestic terrorists.

Someday soon the pandemic will end. Winter rain and snow may cause the rioters and looters to rethink their activities.

Including "rising fears" in the title of this book was not intended to be an act of fear mongering. But is intended to acknowledge that many of us are experiencing more fear than they did at the beginning of this year.

Contrary to the profound words of FDR we have much to fear beside fear itself. Depending on the outcome of the presidential election in November, these are some potential causes of fear in America:

Economy

The longer America is shutdown, the weaker our economy will become. Many people are waiting to go back to work — many have no jobs to return to. Many companies have become zombies and are holding on by whatever means possible. For example, the limited number of restaurants that have managed to stay afloat by often improvised outdoor dining may face new challenges when winter sets in. Pandemic relief programs have been slowed down in Congress. And it will someday be determined that fraud and abuse was extensive. Ultimately the taxpayers will foot the bill and we may be asking ourselves "was it worth it?" Our economy is strong and will survive with the right leadership.

China

We have much to fear from China —
both from an economic and military
standpoint. PRC has ambitious plans
to accomplish over the next 20 years.
China's obsession with global
domination is something that we
must take very seriously. It's a threat
much greater than any that might
exist south of our border.

Domestic Terrorists

Antifa, BLM, and whatever other
groups using whatever names or
fronts will continue to be a bigger and
bigger threat until we can uncover
who is behind these groups and
where their money is coming from.
It's scary when what start as peaceful
well-intentioned demonstrations
morph into violent riots and looting.
Defunding the police and controlling
what equipment they can use makes
no sense when it is apparent that the
domestic terrorists are well-funded
and well-equipped. We must restore
law and order to America at all costs.
Domestic terrorists in America are
not easily identified.

Cancel Culture
We should be afraid of the slow undoing of what we have created over the 400-year American experience. We should be afraid of those who would have us all on our knees begging for forgiveness.

Lack of Leadership
Now more than ever we need a new breed of leadership in America — in all three branches of our government and in the media and private sector. We need leaders who have courage and commitment. Lack of leadership could create a perfect storm for the American Dream to unravel and for the rapid deterioration of our social, political, and economic system. We need leaders who have both short-term and long-term strategies. And, most important, we need leaders who will surround themselves with the best and the brightest.

We cannot allow fear to keep us from ending the pandemic, restoring law & order, and saving the American Dream.

It's fun to be on the edge.
I think you do your best work
when you take chances,
when you're not safe,
when you're not
in the middle of the road,
at least for me, anyway.

— Danny DeVito

FOUR

ON THE EDGE

Leveling society to make everyone equal is not only impossible, it's inherently destructive, it breeds corruption, and it's totally incompatible with freedom and limited government.

— Sean Hannity
Live Free or Die:
America (and the World) on the Brink

Being on the edge can be both good and bad — like a glass half full or half empty.

ON THE EDGE

America is on the edge — but it is not our first time and probably will not be our last. Our nation started out on the edge. In many ways we have always been on the edge. That's what made America great. We are risk-takers. We dance on the edge. We color outside the lines — and sometimes even erase the lines in the process. We reach for the stars — all of them.

The difference with being on the edge now and in other times in our history is that we are starting to buy into the belief that the glass is half empty and going down quickly.

Japan put us on the edge when it bombed Pearl Harbor and the Boston Marathon bombing put us on the edge. We were on the edge before and after December 7th, and before and after September 11th. Most of us can remember being on the edge dozens of times during our lifetimes.

Perhaps the greatest challenge of the president of the United States is to make sure we do not fall apart when we are on the edge— that we do not allow fear to paralyze our hearts and minds. We can — and have — survived bombings because we can rebuild military bases and buildings. Lives can never be replaced and that is why lost lives represent the true cost of terrorism. But we become vulnerable when we allow our hearts and minds to be manipulated. And that is exactly what is happening in America today.

In the depth of the Great Depression FDR assured us that "… the only thing that we have to fear is … fear itself…" in his inaugural address. JFK took control during the Cuban Missile Crisis and mitigated our fear.

We are on the edge. Who knows how long the pandemic will last? Who knows how long people will be rioting and looting? We are on the edge of Fading Dreams and Rising Fears and need to take personal responsibility for getting off the edge and getting America moving again. Individually and as a nation we need to save the American Dream.

I have spent my life
judging the distance
between
American Reality
and the
American Dream.

—Bruce Springsteen

FIVE
SAVING THE DREAM

With a good conscience our only true reward, with history the final judge of our deeds, let us go forth to lead the land we love, asking His blessing and His help, but knowing that here on earth God's work must truly be our own.

— John F. Kennedy

Do you believe that "God's work must truly be our own?" like JFK said in his Inaugural Address? Are you going to save the dream?

S aving the Dream is not solely the responsibility of the President of the United States. Each of us has the responsibility to do everything that we can to save the American Dream.

Antifa, BLM, and the other paid and misguided domestic terrorists rioting, burning, and looting America are not trying to save the American Dream. They are doing everything they can to destroy the American Dream — the slow undoing of our free, democratic, and capitalistic society.

The "demonstrations" held over the past months — over 100 days in Portland — stretch far beyond the most liberal definition of "civil disobedience". The fact that Democratic mayors have permitted the loss of lives and public and private property is entirely inexcusable.

The dreams of many Americans have been destroyed by the pandemic and domestic terrorists. Large businesses will survive because they have the resources and ability to "weather the storm" — and will eventually pass on the costs to shareholders and customers. But the owners of many small and medium-sized businesses have been robbed of the American Dream.

So, what can we do to save the American Dream? In the final analysis it all comes down to our ability to keep the economy going in the right direction. Money is the mother's milk of the American Dream. If we can save the American economy, we can save the American Dream.

Perhaps the biggest thing each of us can do now to save the American Dream is to invest the time and energy required to do our due diligence in researching the candidates and issues in the upcoming election.

And once we know where we stand on the candidates and issues, we must vote because our votes matter — every one of them. Try to vote objectively and not from raw emotions that may later prove wrong. Your vote is a priceless gift.

**Political impotence is finished.
Today is the beginning of the orgasm.
All the people, I promise you,
will feel the orgasm of next year's
presidential election.**

— Vladimir Zhirinovsky

SIX

ELECTION

An election is a moral horror, as bad as a battle except for the blood; a mud bath for every soul concerned in it.

— George Bernard Shaw

Donald Trump and Joe Biden have two things in common — they are both running for POTUS and they are both telling us that this is the most important election of our lifetimes.

ELECTION

This may well be the most important election in your lifetime. What is at risk? Pure and simple — to retain our position as the greatest country in the history of the world or to allow China and Antifa, BLM, and other domestic terrorists to drive us back to the stone age and make us like the socialistic shitholes around the world. (think Cuba and Venezuela to name a couple in our hemisphere — not to mention the Central American banana republics).

Try to be as objective as you can as you look at each candidate and evaluate their qualifications to serve as our president over the next 4 years. Match each candidate with your wish list of presidential qualities. Leave personalities out of your evaluation unless you believe that those characteristics will affect a candidate's ability to perform the duties of the office of POTUS.

There are 19 issues for you to consider along with note pages for your analysis. Decide who best matches your issues.

NOTES

NOTES

Issues

The first duty of a man is to think for himself.

— Jose Marti

31

ABORTION
Ranking: #_____

Abortion

I've noticed that everyone who is for abortion has already been born.

— Ronald Reagan

Abortion is an extremely personal and highly emotional issue that cannot be defined by political lines alone. Religious beliefs play a big part in how many people will vote.

You will have to define how you feel about abortion, what the candidates are saying about the issue, and how much weight you want to give abortion in making your vote. For some people this may be the decisive factor in deciding who will get their vote — it may override political loyalties.

CHINA
Ranking: #_____

China

Have fewer children, raise more pigs. (少生孩子多养猪).

— Chinese Slogan (1979)

Negativity toward China will be a major concern in the 2020 election and one that both candidates will leverage in pursuit of support and votes. Concerns include trade, national security, and human rights.

Candidates may not differ on the principles will most likely differ in their individual strategies on how to deal with China and their abilities to effectively do so. Do not ignore the military threat of China.

DEFENSE
Ranking: #_____

36

Defense

He's not the enemy. Scott, the Joint Chiefs, even the very emotional, very illogical lunatic fringe: they're not the enemy. The enemy's an age — a nuclear age. It happens to have killed man's faith in his ability to influence what happens to him.

> — President Jordan Lyman (Fredric March)
> *Seven Days in May* (1964)

This is a tough one. Who really knows where we stand on defense? There have been times in our brief history that even the POTUS may not have known what was really going on. Think George W. and WMDs. What is China doing? Let us not be caught in a position of weakness. President Clinton closed bases around the world. Let's not let this happen. We must defend America at all costs.

ECONOMY
Ranking: #_____

Economy

History has demonstrated time and again the inherent resilience and recuperative powers of the American economy.

— Ben Bernanke

The biggest impact that a president has over the economy is that of instilling consumer confidence. A president has enormous influence over how investors look at financial markets.

.

EDUCATION
Ranking: #_____

Education

Education is the passport to the future, for tomorrow belongs to those who prepare for it today.

— Malcolm X

The pandemic has placed education in the forefront of the 2020 election. There are many issues— when, where, and how to continue educating America's youth.

Beside the pandemic other topics related to education include school safety — especially since we have rioting and looting in major U.S. cities. Candidates should be addressing teacher's pay, student loans, educational funding, and civil rights issues. Education has changed drastically.

FOREIGN POLICY
Ranking: #_____

Foreign Policy

Most Americans are close to total ignorance about the world. They are ignorant. That is an unhealthy condition in a country in which foreign policy has to be endorsed by the people if it is to be pursued. And it makes it much more difficult for any president to pursue an intelligent policy that does justice to the complexity of the world.

— Zbigniew Brzezinski

Foreign policy includes — but is not limited to — war, foreign aid, and agreements.

GUNS
Ranking: #_____

Guns

To conquer a nation, first disarm its citizens.

— Adolph Hitler

The fear caused by the pandemic — and the rioting and looting — has put the spotlight on gun control. With rising fear, we have seen a significant spike in gun sales. This is a highly emotional issue and voters will be watching the presidential candidates to see what they plan to do.

The frenzy to "defund" law enforcement in the US — and increasing violence will continue to influence how we feel about our need to arm and protect ourselves. What do people think they will do without police?

HEALTH CARE
Ranking: #_____

Health Care

Healthcare should be between the doctor and the patient. And if the doctor says something needs to be done, the government should guarantee it gets paid for.

— Michael Moore

H ealthcare continues to be a major issue again this time around.

HOUSING
Ranking: #_____

Housing

I never doubted I would have a roof over my head, a school to go to, enough to eat, books (and newspapers) to read, a safe neighborhood to play in and a doctor to see if I got sick. My parents and grandparents made sure I knew I was lucky.

— Chelsea Clinton

Affordable housing in America has been forced into the forefront by the economic impact of the pandemic. Providing affordable housing is more challenging than ever because of several factors. Construction has been shut down and foreclosures are imminent for many. Producing viable solutions that will be a challenge for both presidential candidates. The issue is not whether we need housing — it is who can best make it happen.

49

IMMIGRATION
Ranking: #_____

Immigration

A nation that cannot control its borders is not a nation.

— Ronald Reagan

Voters are not necessarily rallied around immigration issued based on political party affiliations, racial or ethnic characteristics, or economic status. Support and opposition are not easily categorized — this is a major issue that could make or break the election. Try to deal with facts — not fiction.

INFRASTRUCTURE
Ranking: #_____

Infrastructure

You know, if you look back in the 1930s,
the money went to infrastructure. The
bridges, the municipal buildings, the roads,
those were all built with stimulus money
spent on infrastructure. This stimulus bill
has fundamentally gone, started out with a
$500 rebate check, remember. That went
to buy flat-screen TVs made in China.

— Michael Bloomberg

Before they became under attack by
rioters and looters America's cities
and rural communities were
crumbling and suffering from decay and
deterioration. We need to rebuild America's
infrastructure like we did to recover from
the Great Depression. Let's build and repair
highways, bridges, schools, hospitals,
airports, and all of our infrastructure.

JOBS
Ranking: #_____

Jobs

The idea of having a steady job is appealing.

— Robin Williams

America needs jobs. Workers have become unemployed zombies and America is ready to get back to work. Tragically many of their jobs have disappeared.

Anyone who can create jobs during this pandemic is a hero. Creating jobs should be the name of the game for both presidential candidates.

FDR put 8.5 million people to work over 8 years with the WPA to rebuild America. Let's do the same as we reopen America.

LAW & ORDER
Ranking: #_____

Law & Order

We shall establish freedom from fear in America so that American can take the lead in reestablishing freedom from fear in the world.

— Richard Nixon

Sixty years ago, Richard Nixon lost the presidential election to John Kennedy. Eight years later Nixon made a dramatic comeback to win the election of 1968. Richard Nixon said that we have a right to be free from the violence of civil unrest. He was elected by "the great majority" of Americans, the forgotten Americans, the non-shouters, the non-demonstrators" — the same profile of voters who will decide 2020. Decide if you want to be the solution or the problem.

PANDEMIC

PANDEMIC
Ranking: #_____

58

Pandemic

Near, far, wherever you are… make sure you're practicing social distancing!

— Celine Dion

Many voters will make their decision based on how they believe that the pandemic was handled — or in their opinions — mishandled.

We will probably never know the truth about what happened and why. And there is nothing we can do about that — the past is the past. We can learn from the nightmare and try to make sure that we are never again put in this situation. How the pandemic was handled will be a big issue. It's easy to criticize after the fact. Who can best handle this pandemic and any future ones?

RACE & ETHNICITY
Ranking: #_____

Race & Ethnicity

I have a dream that one day little black boys and girls will be holding hands with little white boys and girls.

— Martin Luther King Jr.

There is no immediate answer to race and ethnicity issues in America — but we know that rioting and looting is not one of them.

BLM has sucked many people in under the promise of racial equality. Is that the real agenda — or is there a hidden one? Don't allow yourself to fall prey to those who find it easy to put labels on other people. The term "racist" is being tossed around like croutons on a Caesar salad. And it is not an easy thing to defend yourself from that.

TAX
Ranking: #_____

Tax

The hardest thing to understand in the world is income tax.

— Albert Einstein

S omeone has to pick up the tab for the pandemic and rioting and looting — the question — is who's that going to be?

It is going to take someone who is a financial genius — a president who understands both business and economics — to figure out a tax plan that is fair and won't smother Americans as we struggle to financially recover from the pandemic.

TECHNOLOGY
Ranking: #____

_____

_____

_____

_____

_____

_____

_____

_____

_____

_____

_____

_____

Technology

Our technology forces us to live mythically.

— Marshall McLuhan

Protecting consumer privacy is one of the biggest tech issues in the 2020 election along with tech competition and antitrust. China and cybersecurity and tech espionage are major threats that must be addressed.

The pandemic has exposed our dependence on the virtual world along with encouraging technological innovation and creativity. We have discovered new ways to communicate, conduct business, and educate ourselves.

TERRORISM
Ranking: #_____

_____

_____

_____

_____

_____

_____

_____

_____

_____

_____

_____

_____

_____

_____

_____

Terrorism

The object of terrorism is terrorism. The object of oppression is oppression. The object of torture is torture. The object of murder is murder. The object of power is power. Now do you begin to understand me?

— George Orwell
1984

Terrorism as we knew it — the attacks on 911 and the Boston Marathon bombing — have been replaced by domestic terrorists like Antifa and those who are attempting to undermine America under the disguise of BLM. Defunding police and restricting the ability of ICE and other agencies to protect our nation will compromise our national security. Trump will build up our counter-terrorism efforts.

TRADE
Ranking: #_____

Trade

Sooner or later every trade war becomes a war of blood.

— Eugene V. Debs

As much as we might be inclined to shut ourselves off from the rest of the world that is an impossible and unrealistic dream.

Trade with China will continue to decline but will be quickly replaced by increased trade with Latin America. Sixty years ago, Kennedy tried to embrace Latin America and that never happened. The 1994 free trade agreement with Mexico and Canada (NAFTA) was replaced by USMCA — the U.S. – Mexico – Canada Agreement — effective July 1, 2020.

**... and we stand today
on the edge of a New Frontier
– the frontier of the 1960's,
the frontier of unknown
opportunities and perils,
the frontier of unfilled hopes
and unfilled threats.**

— John F. Kennedy
DNC Nomination Acceptance
Los Angeles
July 15, 1960

SEVEN

BACK TO THE FUTURE

If you put your mind to it, you can
accomplish anything.

— Marty McFly (Michael J. Fox)
Back to the Future (1985)

**There is a reason that God did not give us
heads that swivel 360° – so we cannot keep
turning around and look backwards.**

**What America needs to do these days is
:"fuhggedaboudit" (like on the Leaving
Brooklyn signs) – or "fuggedaboutit" (like in
Goodfellas). Let's fuhggedaboudit or
fuggedaboutit and move on.**

Let's get back to the future — the future of America. On January 17, 1925 President Calvin Coolidge gave a speech to the American society of Newspaper editors in Washington D.C. Coolidge talked about the role of the press in free-market America. These words are often misquoted as "the business of America is business." The accurate quote is: "After all, the chief business of the American people is business. They are profoundly concerned with producing, buying, selling, investing and prospering in the world."

Less than six weeks ago we published *C19 Economics: Your Guide to Personal and Business Finance.* Our book presents ways for Innovators, Investors, Entrepreneurs, and Advisors to save the American Dream.

As of the publishing of *Fading Dreams and Rising Fears: America on the Edge* there are about six weeks until the presidential election — the election we are being told will be the most important one ever.This book is intentionally simple and is designed to be an easy and fun read. We are not professional writers or journalists. There are a lot of things we could have included in this book. We are aware that we need to publish our book in time for it to help you make your election decision. And we are aware of the theory of "paralysis by analysis" so we tried to "dumb it down" to sixth grade English. Our biggest challenge, in the words of Bob Seger in *Against the Wind* was "Deadlines and commitments — What to leave in, what to leave out." Like us, you have lived through each and every nanosecond of this nightmare. There is absolutely no reason to remind you of the details of what we have all been through.

We appreciate your investing in our book and hope that you will invest in your own due diligence and vote your conscience.

America is a great country with a great future. You are the magic of America's future — each one of you. Stay safe and remember to wash your hands for lunch. God Bless you and God Bless America.

73

The future belongs to those who believe in the beauty of their dreams.

—Eleanor Roosevelt

WASH YOUR HANDS FOR LUNCH
Robert Miller

The greatest gift God gave mankind was the ability to forget.

— Joe Biden

2020 may turn out to be a year that we all want to forget. Pandemic. Riots. Vicious election. But before we write the year off, let's stop for a moment and think about what we learned.

S omeday, hopefully not too far in the future, the pandemic will be under control. And, someday not too far in the future, riots and looting will stop and law and order will be restored to America.

Perhaps we have placed too much emphasis on the election of 2020. The election has been a cut-throat battle of mudslinging and misinformation — and it will probably continue to get worse right up to the end.

What we learn during the campaign by closely watching and listening to the candidates should be applied to the decisions we make and the actions we take moving forward.

2020 was not the first presidential election for most of us and, hopefully, will not be our last. Regardless of who wins the election, life will go on in America. And, perhaps, we have come to believe that the winner will have the ability to drastically change the way we live. This is what talking heads and politicians want you to believe — not true!

WASH YOUR HANDS FOR LUNCH

What have you learned from the pandemic and presidential election of 2020? For many of us, it has been a humbling experience — one that has taught us survival skills and the ability to survive and (sometimes) flourish in a mainly virtual society.

From the pandemic we have learned how to pivot and improvise, the value of loved ones, and the power of believing in ourselves and in God.

From the election we have learned how dirty politics really can be. We have experienced, firsthand, how politicians and media try — and often succeed — to manipulate and control us.

From the riots and demonstrations, we have seen the danger of mass hysteria and how a crowd mentality can take over.

Without learning from the past we can never change the future. *We the people* should have the power to determine our own individual and national destinies.

WASH YOUR HANDS FOR LUNCH

America is on the edge and we will continue to have *fading dreams and rising fears* until we come together as a nation and decide on a common path to the future.

What America do we want? What America do you want? I want the America of my happy days and wonder years. I want an America where everyone has the ability to earn steak but — at the same time — everyone has hamburger to eat. (And, as a vegan I mean this metamorphically.)

I want an America that's truly color blind and one where mutual respect is not referred to as "tolerance".

I want an America that is sympathetic to world needs and but puts America first. I want an America that produces as well as consumes.

I want an America where we take care of those who are unable to take care of themselves — but do not enable a welfare state that can be exploited .

WASH YOUR HANDS FOR LUNCH

The pandemic has humbled me. Before the beginning of this year, I thought that I had "seen it all". Now I realize —more than ever — how much more I need to learn about people and about life.

This year I have experienced the good, the bad, and the *very* ugly. I pray that God will provide us the strength, courage, and leadership to end the pandemic, restore law and order, and save the American Dream.

More than anything else, the pandemic is a start reminder of our own mortality and how precious every nanosecond of life should be. Embrace life, love those around you, learn to love yourself, and allow yourself to be loved by others.

Whatever the outcome of the election, hold on tight to your dreams — all of them. Reach for the stars — all of them. Continue to color outside the lines — and erase as many as you can in the process. Have no fear and always dance on the edge. And remember to *wash your hands for lunch.*

FEAR IS STUPID.
SO ARE REGRETS.
— Marilyn Monroe

SECOND WIND

THE MAGIC OF MAKING YOUR LIFE GREAT AGAIN

ROBERT MILLER

THE MAGIC OF SELLING

ROBERT MILLER

RAINMAKING

ROBERT MILLER

www.ingramcontent.com/pod-product-compliance
Lightning Source LLC
Chambersburg PA
CBHW070812280326
41934CB00012B/3162

* 9 7 8 0 9 9 7 5 8 8 7 3 6 *